CANNON MINE

poems by

Mary Crosby

Finishing Line Press
Georgetown, Kentucky

CANNON MINE

Copyright © 2019 by Mary Crosby
ISBN 978-1-63534-998-6 First Edition
All rights reserved under International and Pan-American Copyright Conventions. No part of this book may be reproduced in any manner whatsoever without written permission from the publisher, except in the case of brief quotations embodied in critical articles and reviews.

ACKNOWLEDGMENTS

Grateful acknowledgement is made to the following publications, in which some of these poems were first published:

Blueline: "To a Dragonfly"
Dos Passos Review: "Redemption"
Earth's Daughters: "The Ramapoughs"
Narrative Northeast: "The Same Ground"
Paterson Literary Review: "Long Pond Ironworks"
Shot Glass Journal: "After Six Months Unemployed"
The Kerf: "Cannon Mine"
The Turnip Truck: "Stream"

My sincere gratitude to the following teachers, friends and fellow poets for their guidance and wisdom: Chris Salerno, Timothy Liu, Karen Marcus, Edytta Wojnar, Valerie Schermerhorn, Karen Lee Ramos, Joan Page-Durante, Anna Appel, and always: so much gratitude to my parents, Joe and Mary McGhee, my husband John, daughter Sarah, and son John, for their steadfast support, encouragement and love.

Publisher: Leah Maines
Editor: Christen Kincaid
Cover Art: Mary McGhee
Author Photo: John L. Crosby
Cover Design: Elizabeth Maines McCleavy

Printed in the USA on acid-free paper.
Order online: www.finishinglinepress.com
also available on amazon.com

Author inquiries and mail orders:
Finishing Line Press
P. O. Box 1626
Georgetown, Kentucky 40324
U. S. A.

Table of Contents

The Mines 1

Ripple Effect 2

Long Pond Ironworks 3

Forge 4

The Ramapoughs 5

Cannon Mine 7

Occupation 8

Sludge Hill 9

Gaia 11

Writer's Block 13

NJDEP Samples Surface Water at Peter's Mine 14

The Same Ground 15

Superfund Site 16

How Far Removed 17

Out of Waking's Subtle Duststorm 18

To a Dragonfly 20

Augury 21

The Blue Jay Is Looking 24

Clio's Slow Return 25

Mine 26

After Six Months Unemployed 27

Stream 28

For My Parents
&
John, Sarah & John

THE MINES

> *During the 1960's & '70's, the Ford Motor Company dumped millions of gallons of industrial waste into Iron Mines near where the Ramapo Indians resided. In 2005, this tract of land in the Ramapo Mountains became the first site in EPA history to be relisted as a Superfund site.*
> —History of Upper Ringwood, New Jersey

There are poems to be found in these mountains
where Ramapo Indians now reside
on balding lawns beside the town
dump. Ford tires and rusted carburetors
litter the woodline. Sink holes
circled with yellow caution tape
emerge with increasing frequency. Once
a young man standing in his yard
disappeared down a dark shaft that opened
at his feet. His family flashed strobe lights
and climbed down with ropes, calling
his name. Beneath the ground surface
ancient mines sprawl for miles
with uncharted passages, where voices call out
from an alluvian stream.

Ripple Effect

after Yehuda Amichai

The diameter of my diamond
wedding band is seven millimeters

and the diameter of its sparkle
and clarity about a quarter

acre beside a lake
with a three bedroom ranch

a perennial garden nearly always in bloom
and around these in a larger circle

of love and time two children
with your amiable disposition

my ear for music playing
violin and guitar the pluck

and strum of clear strings floating
down the hall and out the open windows

LONG POND IRONWORKS

To feed the fires that burned here, men
harnessed the river then harvested the
forest to forge munitions for three
revolutions
until smoke floated over the studded
hillside and the men migrated west.
                            Now stone
walls from blast furnaces are braced
with timber to hold up their history.
Charred, the waterwheel stands motionless.
But the river gurgles and churns again,
finding its voice to reclaim its course.
In the sandy channels where molten iron
hardened, ribbons of grass now wave in the wind.
Above the rustling trees' applause,
a blue jay squawks an old, endless anthem.

FORGE

A furnace: for heating
and beating into shape.
To fashion or mold.
Form: as in tools, a new
nation. To push
on, make one's way
as in: pilgrims
and pioneers. To create
an alliance, as with natives
and immigrants. Counterfeit:
to imitate or simulate. Reshape
with fire.
Flatten with repeated blows.

THE RAMAPOUGHS

It was evening when he stepped outside
for a smoke.
A faint breeze began to drift
through the valley
hollowed by iron mines, now abandoned
as the natives who rooted there.
The moon only half full,
half-lit the yard where he wandered
with his thoughts
about his uncertain future
which faced him like his mother,
her brown eyes rounding
with expectation,
when without a ripple
the grass beneath his feet
gave way   as a sinkhole

       imploded

the cigarette still
in his hand
as he fell
his own weight
compelling him
downward
as he breached the dark
passageway, the red
ember burning
but emitting no light,
and when he landed
on the soft ground,
the overturned earth received
the impact of his arrival
very gently,

as if sinking into a rumpled quilt
and quietly as the feathers
that filled it,
and the dirt rained down
covering him,
filling his ears, his eyes,
and his nostrils,
so that he could not hear them
when they called to him
looking into the dark
future they had inherited.

CANNON MINE

After the whistle blew, the massive conveyer
belt inside Ford Motor Plant ceased
its motion. Then the night-time assembly line
began in earnest at the building's back door
as blue galaxy and forest green
paint that missed its mark on Fairlanes
and Fairmonts was swept from the factory floor,
channeled into a thick river and poured
into metal drums.

A convoy of dump trucks
laden with this leaden sludge waited
until the moon withdrew her spotlight.
Then they rolled past Black Bridge into the dark
tarpaulin of trees, gears grinding as they climbed
the back road's steep incline. Somewhere a hand
waved them through, toward the pocked
and hollowed hills once mined
to forge shot and shell, so many wheels
churning up dust from the past.
Now the clang as the tailgate opened
and the mob of men loaded
55 gallon drums like bullets
into the mountain's empty chamber.

OCCUPATION

At first no one seems to mind
the trucks dumping barrels,

dead batteries, worn tires,
even as they spot fumes rising

off the pile or smell vapors.
Children love how the paint

swirls like spin art, colors of blood
and the sun they stripe on their skin.

Men wade into the pool
waist high, work boots dragging

as they scavenge for snakes—
long copper wires that fetch $30.

Other car parts they'll sell
for scrap after emerging covered

in muck. By-products of industry spawning
other business. But they are hurrying,

racing to beat the iron
claw that will soon cover everything up.

SLUDGE HILL

In a clearing of trees called The Meadow,
children built wagons

and whispered secrets
the trees would keep

but the river carried
on its silvery back.

They played as dump trucks rumbled in
and especially afterward.

The paint sludge oozed like lava,
hardened into a rainbow

slick rock. One boy decides
to take the hood

off the Fairmont
rusting in the woods,

hike to the top of the mound
of sludge, turn the car-

apace over and climb aboard.
Just as the lid began to shift

with gravity, three more kids
jumped on, and the old Ford tipped

and slid, their ride
quick as a sled on packed snow.

Though it was summertime
and the field bloomed with pokeweed

attracting the birds, the purple black
berries swelling with poison.

GAIA

Though quiet and still, I am not
immovable. I shift from time
to time. There are fissures—
a deep fault I can't explain.

Always the rock, I bear the weight
like the stone robed caryatids
shouldering the load
that someone else constructed.

So many wheels and feet
leave their mark,
so many hands
take what they wish.

Without arms, I cannot shield myself
or reach or strike.
There was a time I tried
to speak

but when I opened
they poured a noxious mixture in,
a waterfall that burned
the pitted tunnel

of my throat and blistered
every vein. But pain
can be absorbed, buried
deep where no one sees it.

I have been holding it
all in, keeping all this poison
down. It is my nature
to be quiet and still

though I am not immovable.
I shift from time to time—
there are fissures.

WRITER'S BLOCK

After the Kung Pao Shrimp
and Szechuan Beef, I break open
a cookie from the small black tray.

The fortune reads: *Desire,*
like the atom, is explosive
with creative force.

I slide the white slip between
the pages of my journal
(small seed in an empty field),

like a survivor
deserted and chill, who strikes
stick to rock for any small spark

or a scientist at the center
of a extensive tunnel
where elements collide:

music, memory
language, image—
in search of the God Particle.

NJDEP SAMPLES SURFACE WATER AT PETER'S MINE

They found benzene and arsenic
they found ethylbenzene,
xylene and chloroethane.
They found lead.
They found nickel, chromium,
cadmium, tin.

They sampled, reviewed
and monitored. They promised
after excavating in '79, the site
was decontaminated. They put Ford
in charge of cleaning up.

In 2005 they found tin.
They found cadmium, chromium, nickel.
They found lead.
They found chloroethane, xylene,
ethylbenzene and arsenic. They found
benzene.

THE SAME GROUND

Just now the swans
are sitting on the frozen lake

as if nesting.
Earlier they had flown in

like a fleet of jets
in military formation

turning when they reached the cove
then opening their enormous

white wings, five parachutes
gliding onto the ice.

What's made them return
north so soon?

The covered ground the same
color as their wings.

Spread out on the lake's
opaque surface they remain

regal chess pieces
poised for their usual move.

It's a familiar pattern—like yesterday
while driving along a customary route

I ended up somewhere
I hadn't meant to go.

SUPERFUND SITE

Who holds the keys to so many
locks

barring the way
to Peter's Mine? Who built

this fence, a silver chain
as if to restrain

the forest? Who
notices the red-ring

milkweed, three feet
high encircling

the long abandoned
backhoe?

Ivy now twining through
the links? The wood's green

tendrils reclaiming the steel?

HOW FAR REMOVED

The other side of town is near
where Ford buried thousands

of tons of sludge.
It's where the Ramapo Indians live

in old miner's cabins beside a river
but that doesn't concern the rest

of the town who don't believe
they're real Indians,

think the mines are far enough
away. They don't look close

to the pictures seen in history books
call them Mineys or worse

based on a legendary war captain.

OUT OF WAKING'S SUBTLE DUST STORM

Gazing out the window at the gray
gray day after weeks of heat
the sky heavy with unfallen rain
no clouds no gradation
of smoky gun-metal thunderheads
rumbling with their booming music
no thrumming of raindrops no
snaredrum of a drenching downpour
just this nebulous gray mass
pressing down

*

You lay on the examining table
shirtless one arm over your head
as if floating on a raft
across a waveless lake

seeing you there
the past is clear again
audible as a voice across deep water

my brother John, skinny
with tousled hair looked
as you do now, my son,
laughing as a doctor presses
a probe along your ribcage

trying to read the grainy gray
screen where your heart swims
& dilates like a sea anemone

*

A covey of doves perches in a row
along the telephone wire
waiting
for the weather to change
or a voice to come through the line

TO A DRAGONFLY

Ancient shape
shifter how you live
for years in the dark
stillness of the lake
happy as a bass with your underwater
breathing apparatus
and how when you are called
to change
you do not look back
at the shimmering world
you'd always known
but instead climb onto a green reed
where you accept this elemental
change without question
where you shed your old self
the now papery
skin and useless gills
where you wait
and warm in the sun not one
but two pairs of wings
until you rise in your new
bright blue body on a column
of air and fly

AUGURY

My daughter does not believe
in signs, that the universe is sending

messages. She studies philosophy
and trusts in reason. Logic.

She wants proof for my claim
about two hummingbirds jousting in mid-

air. The moment I walked down the front steps
and my flip-flopped foot sank

into a gap, and my ankle
folding like an origami swan.

I spent the next four days
in a splint, foot propped on two pillows.

The message: stay home.
That doesn't mean anything

she said. People fall.
I remind her of our ride to Brooklyn

the previous day, when the cars
around us on the GW Bridge

began honking like geese in a V
because they could see what we did

not: a fire beneath the hood.
After I pulled up on the emergency brake

and we bailed from the center lane
rolling fire became a wave

breaching a levee,
as it consumed the car.

When we don't pay attention
to the message, the universe

speaks louder. Stay home
is what I'll have to do without a car.

A freak accident she admits
but not a message.

Today we drive a borrowed car
back to the bridge

to pick up the police report.
While sitting in stop and go traffic

I notice a wing sticking up from the ground.
My daughter is leaving home

for the first time. Going away to college
tomorrow morning.

As we crawl along I see the wind
ruffle the feathers

or did the bird lift its wing?
I peer over the top of the door

observe a pigeon lying sideways
in a sewer, struggling to pull itself

from between the grates, the blue gray
wing waving. In the stream

of traffic I pull over. Sarah and I both
jump out of the car.

I cup my hands beneath him, his wing
slides easily through the wide slats.

THE BLUE JAY IS LOOKING

The snow in the woods has melted
into a small stream between the trees
where a blue jay bows his head
to drink then cleanse his wings.

Though it's mid-January
the south-facing hillside is brown again
with autumn leaves the bird turns over
looking for worms.

Doesn't he know it's far from spring?
Can't he feel the cold wind
cut across the frozen lake?

I wonder this as I sit by the window
in the sun, head bowed,
leafing through the pages
of a seed catalogue.

CLIO'S SLOW RETURN

This morning on the lake
a trail across the water
a way through
but no traveler there

Though the cold wind blows in
from the back door
Winter left ajar
a voice ripples toward shore

In the wake
of the lake's liquid peace
the white scrolls of sailboats borne
by wild breath

MINE

an old   that or those belonging
to me   this land   a deposit   to dig
to extract ore   hundreds of thousands
of tons of iron   an ore zone
red and blue short iron   for wealth
and war   guns   tools   cannons
chains   the great chain
to remove enemies   an old   exploit
erode   extract   precious metal
to undermine   with holes   depression
shafts   tunnels   trenches
to burrow   to hide   depth
charges   ash can   an old ticking
time bomb   not
yours

AFTER SIX MONTHS UNEMPLOYED

But when I turn the paper
right-side up the bold caption
actually reads: *Dream Closer
to Reality*. And I wish it could be
that easy, a simple adjustment
in perspective
when the world seems upside down.

STREAM

> ...BOROUGH PROPOSES RECYCLING CENTER ON SUPERFUND SITE.....
> EPA FINDS 1,4 DIOXANE IN RINGWOOD BROOKS....

At the headwaters I spring
into existence
rise like an idea
from the mountain's mineral mind
glide along
Ramapo's stone shoulders
across the stubbled field
of his broad chest
and enter
every orifice
the metal chamber
of his heart
its muffled drumbeat
branching deep veins
of ore
wash over
open wounds
porous mines from a poisonous past
everything
becomes part of me
and when I come
to the reservoir
in the mountain's lap
comingle with its rich promiscuous
history I become part of
you waiting downstream with cupped hands

Mary Crosby is the author of a previous chapbook, *Alluvium Stream*, published by Finishing Line Press in 2012. Her poetry appears in *Calyx, Narrative Northeast, The Paterson Literary Review, Earth's Daughters, Dos Passos Review,* and *Blueline,* among other publications. Crosby is an Assistant Professor of English at Bergen Community College. She lives in the Ramapo Mountains of Northern New Jersey with her husband John and their two children.

www.ingramcontent.com/pod-product-compliance
Lightning Source LLC
LaVergne TN
LVHW041511070426
835507LV00012B/1481